MANIFESTO

OF A

MADMAN

FOR GOOD

BY: JAY SHERMAN

MANIFESTO

OF A

MADMAN

FOR GOOD

Unrelenting Positivity

Author: Jay Sherman

ISBN# 978-0-578-08918-8

TO MOM AND DAD FOR ALWAYS
BELIEVING IN ME AND FOR HELPING
ME TO BELIEVE IN MYSELF

ACKNOWLEDGMENTS

I want to thank my mom and dad for always pushing me towards my goals and showing me unconditional love as I shove off on this journey called life. Thank you mom for your tireless help with the editing and shaping of this book, without you my message surely wouldn't be as clear; and thank you for helping me to see the positive and teaching me the importance of paying it forward in all aspects of life especially consciousness building. Thank you dad for always motivating me in my writing, asking questions and giving me advice that I will carry with me the rest of my life.

Thank you Chip for telling me I must release my fire and passion onto the world before it's too late. Thank you Ryan, my brother, for being genuinely interested in my work and for always pushing me to be better. Thank you Sean, my brother, my comrade in arms for always being there to bounce ideas off of and proving there are many people out there who are ready for the ideological battle ahead.

Thank you Megan for always being there with a smile, a hug, a kind word and environment healing solutions. Thank you April for your immense positive, beautiful and loving energy and for proving that a person's creativity and passion is what makes their heart sing. Thank you Zeb for showing me how important loyalty is and for making me want to be a better man. Thank you Star for being there through my ups and downs and for teaching me to never lose my consciousness no matter how dark life gets.

Thanks Brent for always being my buddy. Thanks Turtle for proving conspiracy theorists aren't all crazy people wearing tin foil hats, some of them are the most intelligent people anybody could meet. Thanks Woody for always being down to chill with the Critic. Thank you B.J. for being present during some of the most memorable times in my life.

Thank you Tim for being my oldest friend, there is nobody I want to share this with more. Thank you Laurie for opening my eyes, teaching me to always check what has been swept under the rug and pushing me to be a better writer, person and spiritual being. Thank you Ted for proving that Buddhist hippie cowboys do exist and they're some of the nicest people you would ever meet.

Thank you April Z. for showing me what's possible when a person stops talking and starts acting towards their life's passions; I wish you the best of luck on your journey, though I doubt you'll need it. Thanks Bob for being one of the best people I know. Thank you Adam for always pursuing your goals no matter who told you couldn't, and all those Monday night football bets.

Thank you Brad for all the good times, off-roading trips and for knowing what's really important in life. Thanks Daryush for the safety meetings and for the political brainstorming sessions. Thanks Don for the Stater Bros.

and Arrowhead years. Thanks Ed for teaching me to always be skeptical. Thanks to the other Ed for all the positive energy.

Thanks Emily for being my journalism buddy. Thanks to the other Emily for believing in her writing skills as well as mine. Thank you Kenu for showing what a person can do when they put their full consciousness into their daily activities. Thank you Jaime Sue for being my buddy during my M.S.J.C. and "realization" years. Thank you Jaime for proving to me that all republicans aren't all old rich white men, but are beautiful, intelligent and articulate young women too.

Thanks Jared for being my buddy before, during and after the "666 rose lane" days. Thanks John from 206 for the good word and the gardening updates. Thank you Jess for being my friend, my confidant, my shoulder to cry on, my cooking buddy; if only life threw us different pitches. Thank you Johnny for the MPH days, the Stater days and his corps days, Semper Fi good buddy.

Thank you Kasper for being my writing buddy and for always trying to get me to play dodge ball. Thanks Kevin for being the awesome rock star you are. Thank you Kim and Rhonda for being one of the most loving couples I know and for always spreading peace and love. Thank you Laura for showing me what real love is and for being the basis of my comparisons. Thank you Lucy for being the most intelligent, intellectual, funny, warm and sexiest "mofo" I know.

Thanks Mackey for proving stereotypes are caused by ignorance. Thanks Maggie for chillin with me in your early days before you become a famous rock star. Thanks Mark for trying to make positive change and for making a joke I will always remember. Thanks Melanie for providing me the personal motivation to write a book. Thank you Miriam for your beautiful soul and the love it provides everyone you come in contact with. Thank you Nicole for your warm personality, unmatched care for others and that wonderfully evil, but amazingly cute giggle.

Thanks Olivier for doing more with one leg than most people can do with two. Thanks Pablo for your infectious laugh and good heart. Thank you Russ for proving a guy can be loyal, hardworking, love his wife, and at the same time never forget his friends. Thanks Sam for the memorable "Arrowhead Villas" days. Thank you Sara for helping me to let go of many of my inhibitions.

Thanks Nate for showing me a person can always achieve what their mind tells them is possible. Thanks Stephanie for showing me a person can and should always stand up for what they believe in. Thanks Steve for the great times in high school at your dad's place. Thank you to the other Steve for letting me know places like BG actually exist, what it's about, the balance of energy it holds, and how things in its inner sanctum truly work.

Thank you Sue and Mike for proving somebody can live off the land and can provide for themselves, their family and friends with all that the land produces. Thanks Susan for being always vigilant to historical accuracies. Thanks to the other Tim for helping me see the true beauty of Humboldt.

Thank you Lisa for being the greatest boss in the world and my surrogate mom. Thanks Kaytizzle you are awesome, for shizzle my nizzle all over the hizzle. Thank you Tadd for the world problem solving talks. Thanks Tasha for the ego boost. Thanks Lee for proving it is possible for people with diametrically opposed political opinions to find common ground.

Thanks Jose for being a great example and balance of hard work, family and fun. Thank you Kaylyn for being the sexiest housekeeper I know. Thank you Sara for being the other sexiest housekeeper I know. Thanks Debbie, Grace and Leona for the kind words, smiles and the awesome vulgar conversations on our breaks. Thank you Kelsey for realizing what's really important in life. Thank you Carrie, you "really get it".

Thank you Kayleen for being the awesome back talking sister I never had. Thanks Lilly, you prove hard work, vision and focus is the key to achieving what's best for your family. Thanks Aime for being the sexiest front desk lady I know. Thanks John for loving metal and snowboarding at 50. Thanks Steve for the great gardening advice. Thank s Dale for always being there with a joke and a smile. Thanks Mike for always being reliable. Thank you Randy for feeling my pain when politicians do something stupid. Thank you James for your courage, keep fighting the good fight.

Thanks Robert for doing your own thing, and making a living like you see fit.

Thank you Trevor for being the best teacher I ever had. Thank you George for being the best professor I ever had and for ingraining in me the importance of critical thinking and discussion. Thank you Gary for being the biggest Beatles fan I know. Thank you Calkins for being the most entertaining teacher I know. Thank you Horak for being the most patient and motivating teacher I know.

Thank you Mrs. Armstrong for spurning my love of reading. Thank you to Montessori and those amazingly wonderful Sri-Lanka ladies, you taught me diversity, music and how to read at age 3. Thank you M.S.J.C. and H.S.U. for making your students struggle which reveals the hard work needed to achieve their goals.

Thank you Grandpa Mel for the great fishing memories, that old van and the warm sodas you always kept in the back. Thank you Grandma Loraine for always being supportive in the best way you know how. Thank you Grandpa Herman for escaping persecution and anti-Semitism in Poland, then enlisting in the American army and going back to fight the Nazi's in the same place that you escaped from.

Thank you Grandma Yona for escaping persecution and anti-Semitism in Palestine before Israel even existed. Thanks Aunt Suzie for always being loyal. Thanks Aunt Lisa for being a strong courageous mother and writer. Thanks

Cousin Shawna for always pursuing your goals. Thank you Uncle Eugene for your love of and your many years spent working in American manufacturing. Thanks Uncle Garry for your great stories and your never dull personality. Thanks Jack for the great dirty jokes. Thanks Wes and Bev for the early college fundraising. Thanks Ted for introducing me to smoked turkey. Thanks Cousin David for your great earthquake story.

Thanks Rico's Taqueria for the awesome combo plates. Thank you Peter and the burrito truck for a kind word and good food, even if it's at 2:30am. Thanks Banana Hut for your delicious bbq. Thanks Rosa Marias for hands down the best burritos and hot sauce in the entire world.

Thank you College Cove, the clear cut on Fickle Hill, the Marsh, the Lagoons, the Lost Coast, Fern Canyon, the Jetties, the Samoa Peninsula, Clam, Moonstone, Luffenholz, Baker, Trinidad State Beach, the "mail box" trail, the bench overlook, Scenic Drive, the old railroad bridge, the quick Mad River spot and all the rivers in Humboldt, Mendocino, Del Norte, Curry and Trinity counties for being close in proximity to where I live and for always inviting peace, humility, love, visualization and reflection to enter into my soul whenever I allow it to do so. Thank you Strawberry Rock for being the sunny spot above the clouds; thank you all from the bottom of my heart and soul.

Thank you universe for all that I have and all that I will achieve; thanks for giving me the courage and strength to carry on amidst diversity (sometimes self inflicted) to introduce as much peace, love and consciousness to as many souls as I can during my short time on this earth.

Thank you to all people I have met, and thank you to all I will meet in the future. But most of all, thank you for teaching me the most important things in life are to be thankful for what I have and to remind myself to think of that thankfulness in every interaction I have because it builds infinite understanding and consciousness.

MADMAN FOR GOOD

ENTRY#1

2/19/11: 6:00PM

Why is it that some of us don't always think about what we hear or what we say? Is it selective hearing? Is our mind somewhere else? Do we have other priorities? Do we not give a shit? Maybe it's because it's different from anything we've ever heard before; maybe it comes from a reliable, trustworthy source and we don't think to question it. Maybe we think we're too dumb or too smart; maybe we don't look deeply into everything and take the majority of life at face value. Maybe we don't question or take in any of the information that bombards us on a daily basis; maybe we're cynical, maybe we're not skeptical.

Whatever the reason, it is part of my mission to find out. How do we help somebody question, if they've never been skeptical before? How do we help somebody to look for the good in people, if they've always been cynical before? How do we show somebody peace and love is the only way to enlightenment, if they only know war and heartbreak? How do we show them the bigger picture if they're always stuck in survival mode? How do we teach ourselves to love and not to hate?

THAT IS MY MISSION AS A MADMAN FOR GOOD!!!!

MADMAN FOR GOOD

ENTRY#2

2/20/11 – 5:09PM

How are some of us with higher consciousness supposed to relay ideas to someone with lower consciousness?

They have their guns, but are armed with an even more powerful, unflinchingly blind faith in a vengeful, unforgiving but somehow infallibly loving and caring god and believe they have the right to tell others how to live.

They preach freedom and liberty, but show dominance and control. They preach small government and free markets, but show big government control through the curbing of personal freedoms, and a free market that appears on the surface to be free and open to everyone, but is really the opposite and controlled by the most powerful interests dictating on down the food chain, how things should run.

They say one thing and do another. Is this because they talk about things based in theories that have never worked out in reality? Does it go to the clean slate theory that says if we mess things up enough and they all fall apart, we get to start fresh with a "clean slate" and build things in a pre-determined and pre designed image?

Or is it because we actually believe in the strength of man, but need help remembering some people need help; maybe including ourselves?

THIS IS ALL PART OF MY QUEST AS A MADMAN FOR GOOD!!!!

MADMAN FOR GOOD

ENTRY# 3

2/21/11 – 5:32PM

Realizing life's simple pleasures, and finding good people still exist in this increasingly dark world reminds me of why I became a madman in the first place.

I'm a madman for people who find their health insurance won't cover them when they've been diagnosed with a life threatening illness. I am a madman for the immigrants who may have "illegally" crossed a border just to make a better life for themselves and their family only to be caught up in a vast, no-holds barred capitalistic game of cat and mouse that doesn't care who it squashes.

I'm a madman for all people who are persecuted when their only dream is to live free. I'm a mad man for all the native cultures getting destroyed that will never return again, just so some foreigner thousands of miles away can put a few bucks in the pockets of themselves and their closest friends.

But mostly I'm a madman for spreading as much peace, love and understanding as it takes so accountability and humanism fully raise the world's consciousness so high that nobody goes without, everybody is cared for, and the entire galaxy is engulfed in white light.

THAT IS WHY I WILL <u>ALWAYS</u> BE A MADMAN FOR GOOD!!!!

MADMAN FOR GOOD

ENTRY #4

2/25/11 – 5:24PM

Have we returned to a time of the "know nothings" when ignorance was thought to be a good thing?; when going to school and earning a degree, so we could develop critical thinking skills in a chosen field and make a positive change in the world while making a living doing what we love, was seen as a detriment to society?

Certain portions of our population seem to be unconscious souls that think walking the walk after talking the talk, so we could help others do the same is equal to socialism, or an evil walk down the path to communism. They need to realize that some of us need help; or they at least need to feel that real opportunities are out there for all of us including them.

How can some of us be so blind and think that what people like me want is a "utopia"? What I really want is for unconscious souls to stop controlling how others live, and look inside themselves and ask, "is this how I want to be treated; do I want to get shit on by huge, conglomerate corporations looking to exploit everything about me, just so they can put another million in their portfolio, when I'm having trouble paying my rent?"

These unconsciousness souls need to spend time "in the shoes" of the poor, not just put the poor under their shoe;

they need to come around by choice; but if not, they need to be forced by being shown in every interaction that they will lose once the majority of us are able to shake off their distractions and unite.

THIS IS A GOAL OF THE MADMAN FOR GOOD!!!!

MADMAN FOR GOOD

ENTRY#5

2/27/11 – 4:09PM

Will bloodsuckers ever learn? Does the world have to implode, explode or be wiped clear in some other way before they'll see the consequences of their actions? Maybe they're patiently waiting for judgment day? Maybe they are consciously speeding up its arrival?

I think sometimes these "vampires" actively seek an occurrence where the world and everything in it will be wiped away, so they can rebuild it in their own image. In their mind, it's possible to have a perfect world where everybody thinks and acts like they do; a perfect people in a perfect place where everything is perfect. Logically this can only be achieved by wiping the slate clean first.

There is a long history of this clean slate world destroying and rebuilding theory; from Alexander the great, to the Romans, to Genghis Khan, Hitler, Mussolini, Stalin, the Russians and many more. Any existing empires, past empires or fledgling empires that have wanted to exist more than a day and expand exponentially have had the clean slate idea. To create, we must first destroy, maybe they're right, but maybe it's them that need to disappear or be destroyed so happiness can return.

THIS IS ONE OF THE METHODS ILL BE EXPLORING AS A MADMAN FOR GOOD!!!!

MADMAN FOR GOOD

ENTRY#6

2/28/11 – 2:30PM

Everybody likes to talk. I like to talk, you like to talk, we all like to talk. When it comes to action, and actually putting some motion behind the words, the crowd shrinks and many of us become scared; some of us get frightened that the perfect little life we've built for ourselves will be upset if in any way, we rock the boat.

Don't question all the time we're told. Just fall in line, make our specific cog or pull our specific lever that allows the machine to function, and we'll get the house, the car, the trophy wife and the boat with matching jet-skis; we'll get all this as long as we don't question where it came from, or what made it possible. We're told not to look behind the curtain to see the powerless man who is really controlling things; it would reveal the whole idea of their control as an illusion, and wouldnt allow it to be unquestionably absolute anymore.

Once the veil is pulled, the true inner workings will be revealed. It will be ugly. It will be brutal. It will most likely be illogical; but, it will be the roadmap for us to rebuild, restore and replace the wrong actions that have been taken with the right ones. We have to know what we are up against before we can defeat it.

THIS WILL AID IN THE BUILDING OF MY PLAN AS A MADMAN FOR GOOD!!!!

MADMAN FOR GOOD

ENTRY#7

3/4/11 – 8:44PM

The answer to why some of us believe in lies is why some of us don't question. Why we buy into things that are sold to us, and why we vote for officials that on the surface appear to be for the working man, but really are not, is one of the main reasons we are so polarized as a populace today. Some of us have been ignoring the collective needs of others (not to mention our own) for so long, that any whisper of the 3 g's (god, guns & gays) pulls at our heartstrings and controls our every action; even though it directly and completely appeals to our emotions and zero to our intellect, it's no wonder some of us get so riled up.

Now, I'm not taking sides on this, I think some actions taken by emotionally and not intellectually driven people are downright despicable; all I'm saying is I understand, I'm not excusing, I'm explaining. If the seemingly unreachable among us is to even have a prayer of being reached, it will be through un-flinching, no-holds barred, unfiltered, uncensored and unadulterated truth. They must be told exactly like it is with direct, indisputable evidence to back up every single point. Some of us have been lied to for so long by so many different entities, that we can only be reached through truth that is plainly obvious; something that punches us right in the face.

THIS WILL BE ONE OF MY MANY ACTIONS AS A MADMAN FOR GOOD!!!!

MADMAN FOR GOOD

ENTRY #8

3/14/11 – 4:43PM

Is it possible to fully realize our passion? If it is, how do we share it with the world? How do we use it for the betterment of man-kind? How do we know it's real?

Certain groups, or should I say, "a certain portion of the population" can spew so much hate and ugliness, the normal reaction would be to defend ourselves and to spew the hate and ugliness right back at them. This just feeds a cycle with an un-ending whirlwind of nasty energy whose only possible outcome is the total destruction of all parties involved. It is only when we shun the dark and let out such an immense amount of love and light that under the weight of its awesome power, it fully illuminates the darkness causing only positive energy and love to survive.

The difficulty is that darkness and hate feed off themselves, but so do love and light. Luckily, the great thing is that when fully charged and ready to go, love and light are so powerful, they will squash darkness and hate like an ant; because darkness only has a cloak of invincibility. Darkness and hate are actually wolves in sheep's clothing.

AS A MADMAN FOR GOOD IT IS MY DUTY TO BRING US ALL TOGETHER AND RAISE OUR COLLECTIVE CONFIDENCE FOR POSITIVE THOUGHTS AND HIGHER CONSCIOUSNESS!!!!

MADMAN FOR GOOD

ENTRY #9

3/21/11 – 3:21PM

The person that counts most in our life is our inner self. Some of us don't realize it or are too busy, or maybe we think it's dumb, or just a bunch of frou-frou stuff; or we might realize that being pro active in making our inner child our #1, will help sustain us to do what we know we must do. The trick is some of us need help to get along. Some us can't fathom that everything we might be searching for, (that thing or that person that will change everything for us) might have been with-in us the whole time; that the strength, courage and determination that seems impossible or improbable to attain for use in carrying out our life's mission, is really inside us. Sometimes it gets buried, covered, disguised, manufactured, drowned or falls asleep. The trick is to not only discover it, (and this is really important), but experience it at the same time.

There are three steps: #1 realizing this inner strength, #2 experiencing it and #3 sharing it with the world for the betterment of mankind. WARNING!!! #1 and #2 can be combined, or done one after the other just as long as they are accomplished, but #3 must be done immediately afterwards. Realizing and experiencing inner strength and courage without sharing it with the world, is the ultimate waste. We are compelled to share it with all of humanity.

JUST ONE MORE PART OF THE MADMAN FOR GOOD'S STRATEGY!!!!

MADMAN FOR GOOD

ENTRY #10

3/23/11 – 1:05PM

Is it possible for a human being to be in power (or some other authoritative position) and exist without a constant need to expand and extend their power? Do they need to keep expanding their territory and/or sphere of influence like a business that has to keep growing, or it thinks it's dying? Will they ever be satisfied with the amount of power and influence they have, and proceed to make it work better and more for the people?

Will the idea of "I have to keep growing so people won't think I'm weak" always be the norm? Or will the power brokers and money changers see that sometimes existing system's blueprints are structurally sound, and only need an upgrade in their operating procedure?

I'M ON MY QUEST TO FIND OUT AS A MADMAN FOR GOOD!!!!

MADMAN FOR GOOD

ENTRY #11

3/23/11 – 3:34PM

When some us rebel, do we think of the consequences of our actions and all the possible outcomes? Do we ponder what our post-revolution country will look like? Are we tactfully acting out a strategy, or are we coming from some deep seeded emotion or want for positive change even though we don't know how, why, where, what or even when it will be accomplished? Are we acting out of anger, or have we acknowledged the anger, let it go and carefully thought out our actions so as to bring on the most positive result?

When fighting for our survival, whether it is physical, emotional, financial, spiritual, all of the above or any combination, it is important to think before we act. If we act purely out of emotion, it may serve some short term goal, but ultimately it will end in failure.

We must not be afraid to stand up for what we believe in, **EVER**. If we want that long lasting, deep-ceded, ever-lasting positive change and higher consciousness, we must have a plan of attack.

THIS IS WHAT I WILL DEVISE AS A MADMAN FOR GOOD!!!!

MADMAN FOR GOOD

ENTRY #12

3/23/11 – 5:53PM

If changing laws aren't easy, how hard is it to change our thoughts? If making, ending or extending a law is the most ugly, unwatchable and non-sensical sausage making process of them all, what would changing the way we think look like? Is it improbable? Is it impossible or does it take such an immense amount of energy and effort, that one of us acting out of pure love for humanity must have many other like-minded people around us to carry out such a seemingly impossible and unimaginably huge undertaking? Does this kind of faith exist? Does it run through each and every one of us only needing to be awakened and utilized? Will this process take week's seconds, minutes, hours, days, weeks, years, decades, centuries or millennia?

This process starts when we learn to see all living humans as having the same needs as ourselves and when we have true accountability in our elected officials. Then and only then can we accomplish the good that our souls always knew was possible.

ANYBODY WANNA JOIN THE MADMAN FOR GOOD?

MADMAN FOR GOOD

ENTRY#13

3/24/11 – 9:17AM

Will revolutionary ideas and revolutionary acts always come from expected sources? Does evidence build and build until there is no question that a crime or falsehood has occurred? Will we see it coming or do revolutionary ideas and people come from unexpected places at unexpected times for unexpected reasons?

With all the horrible atrocities in the world, it's hard not to be cynical and expect only the worst in everybody and everything; then something happens that surprises us. It might be from a mainstream 24/7 news source that will put anything out there. It might come from one of the station anchors who question the extra B.S. spin put on a story, and shows how it's not really as big a deal as it's being made out to be. Sometimes reporters still do their job and actually uncover and report the truth.

THIS IS WHAT I HAVE TO PROPUGATE, DISCOVER AND ENCOURAGE AS A MADMAN FOR GOOD!!!!

MADMAN FOR GOOD

ENTRY#14

3/24/11 – 12:37PM

When appealing to somebody's intellect in resolving any kind of dispute, what is the determining factor that an intellect even exists in the person? Is the whole idea of an intellect objective, or is it different for everybody; or is it made up of some of the same basic principles for all of us with only slight variations to include the human condition?

We have to assume that most of us are basically smart, but sometimes we are so cynical or get wrapped up in our daily routines and life, that we give off the aura of being ignorant, misunderstood or indifferent to a problem. We might know we care, but we might not be conscious or awake to it. We have to teach ourselves that everything is interconnected, that every incident has consequences and repercussions for us all. We must realize that something that appears on the surface to not affect us, really might. Laws of free speech, freedom and peace can only exist if they exist for everybody.

We have to make sure everybody understands our human, earthly, planetary plight and fight in whatever method is needed.

THIS IS ANOTHER THING I HAVE TO FIGURE OUT AS A MADMAN FOR GOOD!!!!

MADMAN FOR GOOD

ENTRY #15

3/25/11 – 9:55AM

Does the idea of labeling feed the ignorance we all sometimes have, helping us to understand something and trying to make logical sense of it? Is it much like how conspiracy theories spring up, that because life is so complex and seemingly random and chaotic, we try to put situations into terms that our brains can comprehend? Maybe we label to make sense out of something that doesn't make sense; but maybe it isn't supposed to?

Sometimes labels portray an idea for a significant time span, and then another group uses that label and changes its meaning or attempts to. Why must we label anything? Why must we put into language, things that might not be meant to be explained in worldly terms? Some things aren't supposed to make "earthly" sense.

THIS IS ONE OF THE THINGS I WILL HAVE TO REMEMEBER ON MY QUEST AS A MADMAN FOR GOOD!!!!

MADMAN FOR GOOD

ENTRY #16

3/26/11 – 9:15AM

Do some of us give off the attitude that we have certain preconceived notions? Is it something in the way we carry ourselves, the way we dress or the way we talk that says, "I'm okay with this statement," or "I think in this way"?

Maybe these notions stem from some of our old historical biases that linger around and cause some of us to spout off every once in a while. Maybe it's because of a fear of change. Maybe its ignorance or maybe it's because of an impossible view of utopia? Maybe we'll throw out a Nazi reference here or a Socialist or Communist reference there and think it's no big deal, that our ideas have full genuine merit.

What some of us fail to realize is that by using these terms outside of their original historical context, causes those corresponding historical events to greatly lose significance. Saying somebody or something is like the Nazis, Socialists or Communists without actually being so, spreads ignorance exponentially.

THIS IS ONE OF THE THINGS I MUST STOP AS A MADMAN FOR GOOD!!!!

MADMAN FOR GOOD

ENTRY#17

3/26/11 – 12:49PM

What provokes, or should I say motivates us to take the next step and act instead of just talking? What is the breaking point for one of us to act on the things that we know in our heart is true? When is the time that we open our window and yell," I'm as mad as hell and I'm not gonna take it anymore?"

Being neutral is the same as being complacent. By not getting involved, we think that things won't get to us, won't affect us or won't upset the comfortable little rut that we have fashioned for ourselves.

The time when we should get involved is not when we become complacent to the world's problems, but when we feel the unrelenting, unapologetic, unadulterated and undeniable feeling that there has to be something more positive and more conscious out there for humanity, and that we will get there, if we put in the effort. There is some truth to picking our battles, though the ones we choose to get involved in and the ones we choose not to get involved in will forever determine our entire species evolution.

THIS IS WHAT I HAVE TO DECIDE AS A MADMAN FOR GOOD!!!!

MADMAN FOR GOOD

ENTRY #18

3/27/11 – 4:13PM

At present time, as power lies in the hands of a small ruling elite, the collective power of our intellect, caring and imagination is slowly bubbling; it is coming to a boil for those of us who choose to see outside of ourselves and witness how the entire game (matrix, system, machine, whatever you desire to call it) is interconnected. When one lever gets pulled it causes a flap to open, allowing fluid motion to commence.

When it was said "every action has an equal and opposite reaction", it was correctly characterizing all aspects of life whether they are social, political, spiritual or financial.

Why is it that some of us can't get over the fact that other people exist, that there might actually be humans that have the same needs as ourselves? Why can't they get past themselves and observe the huge beautiful world out there? Are they blind or narcissistic?

Is it even possible for all of us to come together as a human race after all the tears and bloodshed that have plagued our history and unfortunately continues to plague our present? Can we get past all that has happened actually, really, truthfully, honestly, for sure no-foolies and peacefully co-exist?

THIS GOES AT THE HEART OF MY MISSION AS A MADMAN FOR GOOD!!!!

MADMAN FOR GOOD

ENTRY #19

3/28/11 – 3:24PM

Are we repeating history because we've forgotten it at the same time were telling others don't forget history or you're doomed to repeat it? Have we lived the mantra of do as I say, not as I do for so long that we actually believe we are doing what we say? Are we starting to believe all the lies and falsehoods we've perpetrated for decades that were meant to control the world's population, but wound up controlling us? Have we become the hypocrite we always thought we were just never having voiced it aloud until today? Are we having our cake and eating it too?

We as humans can't possibly live 100%, 24-7 and 365 on our principles, but we can put our best and most earnest effort forward; we can live as truthfully and honestly as possible. Those among us who know what they're doing and the manipulation they are inflicting, must also realize that this is why they are and always will be spiritually lacking. Why they feel they need to control people's lives and their views, is simply because of an over whelming feeling of insecurity and powerlessness in themselves. Hypocrisy is a dangerous weapon used against those of us who don't question. We all need to question and be skeptical, but be loving and calm at the same time; especially those of us who never have questioned before.

THIS IS WHAT I HAVE TRAINED FOR AS A MADMAN FOR GOOD!!!!

MADMAN FOR GOOD

ENTRY #20

3/28/11 – 4:58PM

If it is not possible for us to live 100% on our principles, is it possible to be 100% ourselves all the time? Is it possible to know who we are and to be that person throughout the whole day's interactions? Is it possible with all the distractions and the bad energy that's out there, to believe in ourselves and our character so much that no matter what the world throws at us and how it tries to change us, we will stand tall and push forward? This is what authenticity is all about.

Maybe we need to do some meditation. Maybe we need to do a hobby, read a book, run or go to the beach to find and figure out our true selves. The government and big business tell us what to do, and what to be. The media, schools and law enforcement tell us what to do and who we should be. Even our parents, family and friends tell us what we should do and who we should be.

With all the forces giving us character control and/or committing character assassination guised as constructive criticism, it's hard to know what to do. We all must learn how to pick through the grossness of it to find the few kernels of truth. We have to pick through the garbage to find the hidden treasures.

THIS IS WHAT I MUST HELP PEOPLE ACHIEVE INCLUDING MYSELF AS A MADMAN FOR GOOD!!!!

MADMAN FOR GOOD

ENTRY #21

3/28/11 – 5:36PM

Do we still have the ability to make each other laugh? Is the ability still within our psyche to just let go and laugh? Will some of us find our way through the spider web of government, business and media because we are able to laugh? Is laughter the catalyst that will break down our defenses we have built up to protect ourselves from the truth? Do we remember how to laugh? Do we really want to?

Some of us are able to look at the bright side of things to help cope with events; to process and disseminate our experiences to our peers. Some of us need help remembering the positive, the good and the humor in life. Things are serious enough out there, the worst thing we can do is attempt to make them more so.

We might laugh when there is an obvious, without a doubt bold-faced lie spoken. We might laugh when an utterance so foul spews forth, that its true ridiculousness is on display for all to see. We might not laugh though when something terrible happens, the negative energy might blind us; but we must never let our positive, true and loving nature be fully overcome. We must learn to laugh.

THIS IS WHAT I HAVE TO REMEMBER TO DO AS MADMAN FOR GOOD!!!!

MADMAN FOR GOOD

ENTRY #22

3/29/11 – 1:04PM

Are fears of big brother government control and socialistic takeover some of us have realistic fears? Did the communists and socialists that actually held sway in this country in the 20s and 30s have the ability to bring on their utopian fantasies? Is there evidence of this? Or is it some extremely elaborate ruse that portrays itself as putting forth its true goals and objectives while demonizing the other side, when in actuality the demonization itself projects and describes exactly how its participants are acting? Is the idea of a rebel being turned on its head?

Maybe some of us are fighting for a world we imagine based solely on theory. Maybe it's a huge response that has been undertaken since the New Deal for those of us that were opposed to it. Maybe we knew it couldn't be overturned all at once, and have been chipping away at all the social and political gains made over the years until there is nothing left. Is one side to blame, or the other? Is it based on fact or fiction?

THIS IS WHAT I MUST FIND OUT AS A MADMAN FOR GOOD!!!!

MADMAN FOR GOOD

ENTRY #23

3/29/11 – 3:15PM

Do those of us who claim libertarian ideas of small government and privacy rights believe all of us deserve such things? Do we believe only a small portion of our population that tows the party line deserves the fruits of their labor? Or does our infighting within political parties, (especially libertarian) get caught up on conservative or liberal politics causing us to be unable to rightly say without a doubt what we or our party stands for?

Maybe some of us yearn to be free from government control only if it involves actions that we undertake. Maybe if it involves something we don't undertake (abortion, prostitution, drug use etc.......) government control is just alright. How can we believe in less government and intrusion in our lives, but be against abortion, gay marriage, and drug and prostitution legalization, the ultimate form of government control telling us how we should live? How can some of us say we believe in something, then when asked to explain our reasoning, it turns out we're really against it? Maybe we think the essence of truth is more important than the realistic evidence of it.

THIS IS WHAT I MUST UNCOVER AS A MADMAN FOR GOOD!!!!

MADMAN FOR GOOD

ENTRY #24

3/29/11 – 3:27PM

Is violent revolution and/or war ever the answer to a lack of freedoms and liberty? What if every peaceful and diplomatic solution has been attempted and exhausted, and the only way to ensure a peoples survival and positive evolution is through violent means; does that make it right? If by violently overthrowing or assassinating a warlord, despot or dictator a population is freed, what's to stop the next group of us that think using massive bloodshed and ethnic cleansing are the most efficient and effective ways to get what we want?

A true peace can only be achieved through peaceful means. If this is true, what do we do when the only visible solution to the current problem is violence? If violence is used and we see it as having been an effective method of fixing problems, what is our motivation to use peace? What if the person or group is not overthrown, wouldn't the violence be tenfold in response?

When Ghandi and M.L.K. talked about peaceful protest and civil disobedience, they were really talking about the importance of critical mass. If we got enough of us together that had peaceful aims through peaceful means, it would overwhelm the need for violence.

THIS IS WHAT I MUST FIGURE THE INS AND OUTS OF AS A MADMAN FOR GOOD!!!!

MADMAN FOR GOOD

ENTRY #25

3/30/11 – 1:09PM

What is it in some of us that makes us stand up and say no more, this isn't gonna happen on my watch? What gives us the inner strength, personal will and confidence to know that what we feel in our heart is the right thing and worth fighting for? How do we take this confidence and instill it in others so it helps bring on a positive, social, and political critical mass? How do we awaken our souls to all that is happening around us and say hey, this isn't right and I'm gonna work to positively change my life and the lives of all other beings on the planet?

Maybe we need to figure out our purpose on this earth and the path we're going to take to achieve it. We all take different paths depending on our life experience, environment, interests, upbringing and purpose; as long as all these paths lead to the same place of loving white light and enlightenment, it doesn't matter what path we take because we will have served our purpose. One of the great things about our planet is that it's so diverse with so many different cultures and lifecycles, everybody and everything brings something different to the table. If we all listened to our souls and carried a message of peace and consciousness down our personal, purpose driven and correct path, then critical mass would be achieved.

THIS IS WHAT I HAVE TO HELP BUILD AS A MADMAN FOR GOOD!!!!

MADMAN FOR GOOD

ENTRY #26

3/30/11 – 3:22PM

When a court makes a ruling or issues an injunction, is it explicitly implied that all concerned parties will abide by it? Is it expected they will either follow the new law, (even though they might disagree with it) or will disagree with it wholeheartedly and appeal all the way to the Unites States Supreme Court? Might it also be a possibility that a government figure will not agree with a judge's decision to stop a law from being published and enacted, then turn around and publish the law anyway and begin implementing it, even if it's through very obscure and vague procedures?

If a judge sees that their ruling isn't being followed by the elected official that is supposed to follow it, what is their recourse? Should the person be fined, censured, recalled or reprimanded? Should the official be arrested even if they are presently holding that elected position? Does holding public office mean you are above the law? Does it mean you can rule by fiat?

The appeals process is there for an important reason, redress of grievances; but, if after all the appeals have been exhausted, and the accused official or group still doesn't follow the judge's decision, even if they are presently holding an elected position, they must be arrested, period!

THIS IS ONE OF THE THINGS I MUST FIGHT FOR AS A MADMAN FOR GOOD!!!!

MADMAN FOR GOOD

ENTRY #27

3/30/11 – 3:34PM

Is equality, liberty, freedom, peace, justice, the pursuit of happiness and accountability an unalienable right given to us by God or whatever we believe or don't believe in? Is it given us by the founding fathers through a very important living document called the constitution? Do all of the aspects that make up the human condition need to be earned and fought for, or are they just one more thing we as humans have come to expect be handed us on a silver platter? What is reasonable? What isn't?

We fight wars, have skirmishes, carry out police actions, create religions, articulate arguments, bring out a peace keeping force, we might even bring special forces or "security contractors" to make these obvious aspects of the human condition available to a greater portion of the population. These tactics of trying to fix everything "the way we want it fixed" have been used since the beginning of time and will continue to be used until we as the human race see each other as all having the same basic needs and wants as each other. Will there come a day when fighting or warring for peace and justice will be a distant memory because will be living in peace? Will we be able to pick up our fellow humans and not tear them down?

THIS IS WHAT I MUST FIND OUT AS A MADMAN FOR GOOD!!!!

MADMAN FOR GOOD

ENTRY #28

3/31/11 – 9:14PM

If an elected official's platform is based on the idea that government doesn't work and is the source of all our problems, then doesn't urging or bringing on a government shutdown play right into their hands? By making sure the government doesn't have enough revenue to function (ensuring all the cash and taxes come from the bottom of the income scale instead of the top) aren't they simply proving their point? Aren't elected officials simply doing what the voters who supposedly elected them (or the funders that funded them) wanted them to do?

Maybe some of us don't realize that government will never work right if we keep electing people who say it will never work right. Maybe we think that government is best when it governs least; maybe we're afraid of big brother coming down and telling us how to run every aspect of our lives.

Here's the rub, government officials who say government doesn't work and only has a possibility of working when it's small and insignificant, usually institute (or attempt to institute) more rules which means more control. They play politics with the lives of all the people they say they're protecting, while they only protect a chosen few.

THIS IS ONE OF THE THINGS I MUST STOP AS A MADMAN FOR GOOD!!!!

MADMAN FOR GOOD

ENTRY #29

3/31/11 – 12:33PM

What if an elected official lays out a law they want passed along with all the funding sources, restrictions and implementation procedures and the law fails, do or should they keep trying to pass it? Should they let it be?

What if the next elected official to take their place or some other official from a different area of government all together proposes basically the same law, but happens to be from a different political party than themselves? Does the law or bills original sponsor neglect to support it simply because their political adversary is suggesting it? Do they buck their party, support the realistic, truthful and authentic will of the people, and vote for the law even if their poll numbers might suffer?

In our present political climate of seemingly impossible to overcome party divides and permanent campaign tactics, is it even possible for an elected official to vote their conscience without fear of losing major donors for the next election?

If candidates made sure they governed the same way they campaigned, and utilized pragmatic solutions to vote for things they support, an opposite party proposal wouldn't be as hard to ingest.

THIS IS WHAT I HAVE TO FIGURE OUT AS A MADMAN FOR GOOD!!!!

MADMAN FOR GOOD

ENTRY #30

3/31/11 – 12:47PM

Does playing to a base when seeking political office help out the electorate as a whole, or does it play right into the hands of the major big money donors on both ends of the political spectrum? If these respective political bases seem to have completely different agendas, why a majority of the time do they have the same big money donors? Do these donors not care what party gets elected so long as their needs are met? Is this why some people see the Republicans and Democrats as two heads of the same monster? Is this also why it's scary when these opposite schools of thought actually agree on something, albeit for completely different reasons?

Maybe it's the money that makes these candidates win; I mean when has a poor candidate ever won an election to any office? When somebody is so far to one side, they have more in common with their opposite, than with all the people in the middle.

Having a political base isn't a bad thing; they do help put good ideas forward. But when these wants overshadow what the general public wants, we have a major problem.

THIS IS WHAT I MUST ATTEMPT TO FIX AS A MADMAN FOR GOOD!!!!

MADMAN FOR GOOD

ENTRY #31

4/1/11 – 9:47AM

Will our world exist one day in some form that at present time boggles the mind? Will it change physically, metaphorically and/or emotionally? Will it stay the same?

Our world seems to be constantly changing whether it is for the better or for the worse, most often creating positive and negative aspects at the same time just to make sure were on our toes. All the positive change we feel in the deepest depths of our soul, is it real? Is it happening now? Will it happen in the future? Will it happen at all?

The old saying goes there's no sure thing in life except for death and taxes; well, we should add "change" to the list. We need to get to a point in our human evolution where we not only embrace change, but expect the unexpected. "The only constant is change..............................."

When a major positive change is attempted the people on the con side usually either don't want it, or are afraid of it because it is so different than anything they've ever known before. The most important thing we can all do is roll with the changes and continue to move forward.

THIS IS WHAT I MUST LEARN AND TEACH AS A MADMAN FOR GOOD!!!!

MADMAN FOR GOOD

ENTRY #32

3/31/11 – 12:31PM

When the media produces a news story, is the public version of it, what actually happened? Is it a straight robotic reporting of the facts? Or is it an amalgamation of influences made up of government officials, military, various spy agencies, the FCC, network execs, advertisers, corporate America, editors, publishers, section heads and writers who all decide what story is covered and how? Is it possible to be 100% completely objective while living in the human condition? Is it that amalgamation of influences, the human condition or some other unseen and unknown force that contributes to this impossible act of being 100% objective all the time? Or is it a combination of all three?

There are many reasons why the media might not get a story right, or why an event happened. It might be the 24-7 news cycle and the gutting of foreign bureaus that cause a news outlet to release a story before it's been totally investigated. It might be because so many of us have undiagnosed ADD that our attention span can only be held in short, non-intellectual, emotionally appealing and action packed sound bites. It might also be because we are skeptical of the truth, and have become cynical because we've been lied to for so long.

THIS IS ANOTHER THING I HAVE TO FIGURE OUT AS A MADMAN FOR GOOD!!!!

MADMAN FOR GOOD

ENTRY #33

4/2/11 – 9:15PM

Are we ever truly free? Are we ever free from the never ending vicious cycle of unconscious, non-intellectual and violent reality? Even if we evolve to the point where negative energy, negative people and negative actions are truly shunned and made so insignificant that they have zero influence on anybody or anything, will they disappear? Is a perfect world possible, or is it perfectly impossible?

There is a concept of balance that keeps everything within the human condition in working order. Whether it's described as good vs. bad or negative vs. positive, there is a balance of energies and actions that help keep our collective life experience within a realm we can comprehend. There also might be outside forces at work we can't comprehend that cause us to question whether we truly have free will.

The ability to be free in mind, body and spirit lies within all of us. Attempts might be made to control these things, and they might gain control of our bodies; but they will never, ever gain control of our minds or our spirits unless we let them. We must free ourselves from ourselves.

THIS IS A DISCOVERY I MUST MAKE AS A MADMAN FOR GOOD!!!!

MADMAN FOR GOOD

ENTRY #34

4/2/11 – 1:00PM

We all know the phrase "nice guys finish last"; does it ring true in the political world as well? The way our whole structure is designed and maintained, is it even possible for a genuinely nice person who truly and honestly cares about the entire world's population, is it even possible for them to be elected to major political office? Would they be able to measure up during a head to head debate when their opponent is viciously attacking them; would they be fully able to articulate their thoughts, views and platforms in such a way that everybody understands them? Or are they doomed to a life of always wanting to act and knowing exactly how to do it, but are stuck talking endlessly about their solutions on the microscopic chance that one day they might be instituted?

Being a nice guy or a nice woman is never a bad thing. Let me repeat, being a nice guy or nice woman is <u>NEVER</u> a bad thing! When negativity seems to have overpowered every aspect of our bureaucratic and political world, it's hard to see how a nice person could get ahead, or even get elected. But maybe a genuinely nice person is exactly what we need; somebody who overcomes any hate with love, and breaks the cycle of negative tear-down politics; somebody who only knows peace, unable to comprehend anything else.

THIS IS WHO OR WHAT I MUST FIND AS A MADMAN FOR GOOD!!!!

MADMAN FOR GOOD

ENTRY #35

4/2/11 – 1:12PM

Are we witnessing the end of humanity when all the "crazies" start coming out of the woodwork? Is it the end of civilization when violence occurs with no end in sight, just an increase in severity? Is it the end of the world and life as we know it when there are countless wars, battles and skirmishes going on at the same time in many different parts of the world for the same basic reasons? Or is it the start of something bigger and more positive? Is it just evolution?

Some of us will talk about 2012 the same way we talked about Y2K. Some of us will obsess over being prepared for the day when it all comes crashing down on our heads; but what if a major consciousness shift happens instead? What if all these fights and battles are being fought so people who have lived for decades under brutal oppression can simply live free? What if there are some serious changes happening and all we need to do is accept that things will always change and just roll with them?; because some of us just don't want to be brutalized and ethnically cleansed anymore. Will we be on the side of bettering all humanity, or on the side that fears change and will fight tooth and nail to stop it?

I MUST BRING MORE PEOPLE TO THE SIDE OF POSITIVE HUMAN EVOLUTION AND HIGHER CONSCIOUSNESS AS A MADMAN FOR GOOD!!!!

MADMAN FOR GOOD

ENTRY #36

4/4/11 – 1:14PM

What if giving up old habits is the key to finding the happiness that keeps eluding us? What if trying a different method, breaking up an old routine or mindset or thinking and acting in a different way sets us on the correct path to find happiness and fulfillment? What if our hearts and our minds are strong and prepared for the upcoming ideological battle for the sake of all humanity, but we're using the same old methods that have failed us time and time again? Should we change our ends by changing our means of getting there, or should we suffer through the same old tactics of one time protest and redress that won't move us one inch forward from where we are now?

Maybe the answer lies in keeping up the pressure, in not giving up after one day and thinking a "symbolic" redress of grievances is all that's needed. Maybe we need to break out of these molds that have been constructed for us by a system that says we must stay in line, we must not rock the boat and we can't complain or bring something important to light because of an instilled fear of having the whole system eat its self from the inside out. What if this is the ultimate habit we must break to achieve collectively higher consciousness and happiness levels we have only dreamed of?

THIS IS WHAT I MUST FINDOUT AS A MADMAN FOR GOOD!!!!

MADMAN FOR GOOD

ENTRY #37

4/4/11 – 1:37PM

There is strength of will that lies within each of us that allows, encourages and in some instances facilitates the positive energy, results and consciousness we all crave. Some of us have a farther journey to travel to get even some semblance of positive thought. Some of us have less distance to travel; some of us are already there.

When it's said that the power to achieve our hopes and dreams are always within us, (just needing to be awoken and/or stirred to spring into action) it means simply that; that we presently have and always have had the ability to be our own worst enemy and our own worst critic. We also have always had the ability to be our own biggest cheerleader and biggest motivator. It is a balance between these positive and negative forces that are constantly evolving; requiring passionate vigilance to learn and respond to their design and functionality.

Once this balance is observed, it proves time and time again with mounting evidence that we have the uncanny ability to destroy as well as create. Once we discover we have the power to choose our own path, we will see everything that is laid before us; are we ready for that as a people, nation, and as a planet?

ANOTHER DISCOVERY I MUST MAKE AS A MADMAN FOR GOOD!!!!

MADMAN FOR GOOD

ENTRY #38

4/4/11 – 2:01PM

"Is there something happenin in here, what it is aint exactly clear", but it is right there for us all to see and for all of us to pick up on. Sometimes there is a strange undercurrent that we think is surrounding a certain event or interaction we have, and we just feel that something else is there, that something else is going on; something just under the covers that seems to be pulling all the strings, we just can't make out what it is, or what it means, but we know with our entire being it is there.

Maybe we need to be more open or in tune with the moment to pick up on it. Maybe we could be more analytical and scientific to pick it up. Maybe we could be more creative and intuitive to pick it up. Whatever the solution, there is only one guarantee; it will be different for everybody because of different living experiences.

Some people might reach this stage of realization by paying more attention to the news or reading more. Some people might think outside the box, or think more by the book. The point is the public version of a story is not usually what actually happened. We all must find our own way of deciphering the cobweb so we can discover, inform about and alleviate "what's happenin in here"

THIS IS ONE OF MY GOALS AS A MADMAN FOR GOOD!!!!

MADMAN FOR GOOD

ENTRY #39

4/4/11 – 2:26PM

So what exactly are we fighting for? Are we fighting for the rights of all us to live in peace? Are we fighting for the freedom of oppressed people? Are we fighting for truth in an unending tsunami of lies? Are we fighting for love when all messages spew forth nothing but hate? Are we fighting for understanding amidst an overwhelming amount of misinformation, specifically designed to confuse and distract us so we can't unite and rise up?

Are we fighting for that day when all of us can say with a straight face, there is nobody that lives worse than me? Are we fighting for people who are hungry and have no clean and healthy food, for people who are thirsty and have no clean water, for people who have only rags for clothing, for people who are cold and have no warm and safe place to lay their head at night? Are we fighting for the idea of happiness for all, but only a reality of it for some? Are we fighting so those of us who have more can have much more, and those of us who have less can have even less though that might be unimaginable?

We must define who and what we are fighting for, so we always have the knowledge to motivate ourselves of our ultimate purpose when times are bleak; we must remember why, before we can figure out how.

THIS IS WHAT I MUST DECIPHER AS A MADMAN FOR GOOD!!!!

MADMAN FOR GOOD

ENTRY #40

4/4/11 – 2:45PM

Is it possible for ingrained familial, generational, institutional and deeply held ideas to be changed or amended? Is it within our human experience and our short time on this earth to change the course of history and change the tides? Can we affect the evolutional nature of the world and the environment we live in? How long might it take us to achieve some balance in not only physical and financial realms, but spiritual and mental ones as well? Will it happen before the world implodes? Will it happen way before the end of days with plenty of time to spare, or happen at the last second like defusing a bomb in an action movie?

We must work towards all the goals we carry within us of human betterment and advancement as soon as possible. We must put every idea on the table; we must design a plan of attack and we must carry it out. We must also not get discouraged if positive results don't come as quickly as originally intended.

We must fill our souls and minds with as much consciousness as possible so we can carry on through for the long haul. Healing the planet and changing peoples' way of thinking for the betterment of us all is a long, slow process, but if we hope to succeed, we must prepare for what lies ahead.

THIS IS WHAT I MUST HELP INSTILL AS A MADMAN FOR GOOD!!!!

MADMAN FOR GOOD

ENTRY #41

4/4/11 – 3:21PM

Is there any importance in naming a struggle? Does it matter if there is a bright light and flashy name describing and/or titling a movement? Does a name encourage more people to join and support a movement, or does it turn people off for the same reason?

Does it help with the marketing, advertising, distributing and consuming of a collective action, or does having a name hurt by allowing any and all people to know of its existence?

Giving a name or titling a movement or revolution can bring in massive amounts of participants who will help build it up towards that highly sought after goal of critical mass.

It could bring in people who otherwise didn't know or didn't care about the movement, who might be very active and passionate participants.

We also must realize it can cheapen the whole purpose of a movement by naming it and putting a label on something we couldn't possibly know the outcome of.

By putting a "label" or name on a struggle, we could be putting an expected and calculated outcome on something that has always had the possibility of becoming so much bigger and so much better than we could ever fathom.

We have to walk a fine line in what we name our positive "actions" or "movements," and remember its always more important how and why a movement is happening, then what it happens to be called.

THIS IS WHAT I HAVE TO REMEMBER AS MADMAN FOR GOOD!!!!

MADMAN FOR GOOD

ENTRY #42

4/4/11 – 3:42PM

We must remember our collective needs and our individual needs are often different and might not be mutually exclusive, but it doesn't mean either one should be ignored or discredited. What would happen if we ignored all of our individual needs, wants, desires and thoughts in favor of the collective group, and only what would grow, enlighten and prosper the entire group? What if we only made important our individual needs and wants as vital to being human and living life over the groups needs and wants which would cement the idea of the personal spiritual journey?

Do we go it alone, or do we band together? Do we always believe only critical thinkers (who see their own place in society and revel in it) can save humanity? Do we believe that only when all of us as individuals group together can we create enough positive energy to solve these problems despite their colossal magnitudes?

Some people say one person can't change the world; well, if we all believed that then nobody would ever change anything. It takes many "one persons" to band together to create enough force to fight back. It's about seeing the group and the individual as equally important partners in the game of life.

I MUST RECTIFY THIS AS A MADMAN FOR GOOD!!!!

MADMAN FOR GOOD

ENTRY #43

4/4/11 – 4:01PM

When we look ahead and try to figure out what's going to happen down the line by deciphering what's happening in the present, are we going after a lost cause? Is it possible for us as humans with all the weaknesses and/or liabilities that come with being human to actually figure out everything that's going on right now? Is it even plausible that any one of us living and breathing could know how, why, what, where and when something happens? Is looking at the bigger picture the only sure fire method for deciphering the present or can we skim through and look at everything, picking and choosing what we actually take in?

When we try to make the world a better place, it is important to have a strategy, a plan with the right tactics that will help us achieve our goals. If we want to improve our situation, it is important to know the scope of the problem or we won't know what solution will work. None of us are robots, so the chances of somebody knowing all the reasons that present realities are the way they are is pretty slim. The key is to put the most earnest and true effort forward and pick up as much information and tactical improvements along the way as we can; that way when we do act to better our collective future, we can do it knowing we gave it our 100% unbridled best effort.

THIS IS WHAT I HAVE TO GATHER AS A MADMAN FOR GOOD!!!!

MADMAN FOR GOOD

ENTRY #44

4/4/11 – 4:19PM

Is love really more powerful than hate? Does positive energy have the stamina and determination to overtake negative energy? Is there a fight between the two to see who will rule the kingdom and subjugate the other? Or is it a process of organization, so they can balance each other out leaving only a neutral residue behind? Is all this just some false characterization designed to control the masses by using some other sinister means? Is what we feel and what we see different for all of us, so as to create our own unique realities?

The only way it might be possible to figure out if positive or negative are stronger and more beneficial than the other is through the life experience of trial and error. We sometimes have to try positive and negative solutions to see what will cause a better outcome.

Go ahead, try it, put something positive out into the world and see what happens; then put something negative out there and see what happens. When all is said and done, doing negative things for positive reasons doesn't make sense, but doing positive things for positive reasons is the true way to enlightenment.

THIS IS WHAT I MUST LAYOUT AS A MADMAN FOR GOOD!!!!

MADMAN FOR GOOD

ENTRY #45

4/4/11 – 4:35PM

How do we build up our positive energy and prevent ourselves from "falling asleep" to what's going on around us?

How do we tell ourselves that even though the fight is long and collective peace might be a far off cry from our present state, that positive outcomes happen for those who act positively?

Do we tell ourselves that protests are effective and we should work to build movements, or that the fight is too big and we shouldn't even try? Do we give up or press on?

We all have a collective inner struggle of what we are supposed to do with our lives. Figuring out our life's purpose is the first step in achieving our goals.

We must realize that since all of us are unique, we need to utilize different paths and solutions to achieve the same ultimate goal of higher consciousness.

None of us learn the same way or understand the same as each other. We must find the right path that will work with us. We must figure out on our own what the ends are so we can figure out a means of getting there.

As long as we have a true heart and an honest soul, we will achieve higher consciousness; once all of us experience our own version of this, then all our collective consciousnesses will lead us along the path towards enlightenment.

THIS IS WHAT I MUST REMEMBER AND INSTILL AS I EMBARK ON MY LIFE'S MISSION AS A MADMAN FOR GOOD!!!!

MADMAN FOR GOOD

ENTRY #46

4/5/11 – 1:08PM

Everything that has happened in the past and everything that is happening now, will affect everything that happens in the future; which side will we find ourselves on? Will some of us be on the side of rich and corporate citizens only believing that by increasing their income and decreasing their regulations and taxes are the only ways to fix our problems? Will some of us be on the side of the poor and working class only believing that by increasing their income and increasing regulations to ensure their equality is the only way to fix our problems? Or will some of us fall in between these two polar opposites only believing a combination of benefits for the rich and the poor is the only way to solve our problems?

Maybe choosing what side we are on will better prepare us for the battle ahead; but maybe, just the idea of drawing lines and sides will disconnect us from each other and prevent us from achieving our collective human goals.

Maybe, we will pick sides and maybe we won't. The important thing to remember is that we fight for everybody's benefit, not just our own.

THIS IS WHAT I MUST ETERNALLY INSTILL AS A MADMAN FOR GOOD!!!!

MADMAN FOR GOOD

ENTRY #47

4/5/11 – 3:39PM

Now is the time to act, not tomorrow, not next week, not next year, but right now. How long are we going to let the privileged few of us tell the vast majority of us what to do? How long are we going to let the super rich corporate elite pay little or no taxes, while the rest of us see our rates go up? How long are we going to let these "moneychangers" gut the very programs and unions that built a middle class and brought so many of us out of poverty? When will we say enough is enough and lean out the window and yell, "I'm as mad as hell and I'm not gonna take it anymore", and then act on it?

There is a time and place for everything. If we ever had a time that was ripe for action, it is this moment right now. If we ever hope to live out the dreams of peace, we feel in the deepest depths of our soul, we must act now. We can't wait anymore for that perfect solution to fall out of the sky. We can't wait for the other side to come around. We have to do what we know is right and defend it because it's for the betterment of all humanity. This is an ideological war; don't be caught on the wrong side of history.

THIS IS WHAT I HAVE TO REMIND PEOPLE OF AS A MADMAN FOR GOOD!!!!

MADMAN FOR GOOD

ENTRY #48

4/6/11 – 1:18PM

I talk to people all the time; they tell me times are rough. Times are rough for me, they are rough for all of us; let me correct myself, they're rough for all us except the top 1% of income earners that "earn" the vast majority of <u>all</u> the income in this country. We are all in this together. When one of us is hurting, we're all hurting. When is enough, enough? When will we realize that the positive change we are all desperately seeking won't come from some outside source, it will come from within us? When the day comes that we have the courage to wake up that determination within, there is nothing that the top 1% can do.

Sure, they'll say were a bunch of agitators, terrorist, communist, pinko, socialist, good for nothings just wanting to stir up trouble. We know the truth, and soon they will too. We will use the full breadth of our energy and consciousness to overtake their hypocritical hold on power and show them what happens when the vast human race has full control over their destiny.

THIS IS WHAT I MUST DO AS A MADMAN FOR GOOD!!!!

MADMAN FOR GOOD

ENTRY #49

4/6/11 – 3:35PM

What is the one thing that will sustain us for the long struggle ahead? What is the end all be all answer that will change all those closed minds out there? What will cause them to think everything they've been doing up until this point might be wrong, and they should do things differently, think in a different way or take advice from a different inner circle? Will the same idea or plan help the vast majority of us band together, forget our differences and fight side by side in the long upcoming ideological battle of wills? Or will it be different for everybody at every stage for all sorts of different reasons?

What could help bring us all together is realizing that we all have the same basic needs; we all want to be free, see our children grow up in a healthy and opportunity filled environment and have the peace of mind that can overcome whatever stresses life presents. This is one thing that is easy on paper, but becomes very messy when implemented. Those of us who understand what our true human purpose is will band together, and those of us who don't, will not disappear, but will be made insignificant under the weight of the progressive march of history.

THIS IS WHAT I'VE TRAINED FOR AS A MADMAN FOR GOOD!!!!

MADMAN FOR GOOD

ENTRY #50

4/6/11 – 3:47PM

We must never forget the reasons why we are involved in such a huge undertaking as raising the world's consciousness. We must never let unjust laws rule our daily lives. We must never engage in such individualistic activities as to forget our collective needs. At the same time, we must never forget that as individuals what we do will influence the group and will prevent group speak and blind faith from ever having control over us.

When we shake off all the distractions placed on us and achieve higher consciousness (which will happen, when and not if, when we awaken to all its possibilities) we won't even be able to fathom engaging in unjust wars, unfair financial practices, genocide, ethnic cleansing, religious, racial and sexual orientation oppression and all other negative actions holding back our evolution as a species. We will talk to our neighbors, have faith in our elected officials to do the right thing and will be able to eat and grow healthy and good food knowing all of us have enough to eat and grow without corporate tyranny.

Is this all a pipe dream, just some hippie liberal's utopian fantasy of a perfect world? We will never know unless we make the attempt.

THIS IS MY MISSION AS AN UNRELENTING MADMAN FOR GOOD!!!!

MADMAN FOR GOOD

EPILOGUE

4/8/11 – 11:35AM

If the beginnings of an ideological battle are currently underway that seems to only get more entrenched over time, what do we do? If some us have ideas and beliefs that are diametrically opposed to each other, how can we ever expect a compromise?

The question becomes how can we as a people start to think in a different way? How can we convince others in this country and around the world that all of us have the same human needs as each other? How can we be taught to think outside the box, if we only know inward thinking?

I don't claim to have all the answers, nor do I think some other singular person in our society has all the answers. What I do know however, is that the path we are presently going down is totally unsustainable and will result in our evolutionary destruction. I can see how a portion of us don't and won't think this is happening, because we don't believe evolution exists in the first place; these portions of us will be the hardest to convince.

What if these hard to reach parts of our population are a lot closer than we might think (like a car's rearview mirror that says objects are closer than they appear)? What if they agree with the rest of us on most things, but it's the moral and ideological ideas (gays, god, guns, taxes, the size of government, evolution, etc.......) that are holding them back. If they could just be told that their evolution, existence, human nature and dreams of peace are being blinded, distracted and put to sleep by these moral questions, and that they are keeping them from uniting, than my mission as a "Madman for Good" would be a lot easier. Unfortunately it's not that way; they have to be convinced through unadulterated truth. We have to work together, if we ever hope to have a chance at a better world.

We have to come to a place where we all realize love is hard to come by; and with so many negative experiences occurring in the world, why shouldn't we be able to marry whomever we want if we are lucky enough to find love? We are obliged to arrive at a place where all of us realize that although we might believe in god or a certain religion, not everybody believes the same way we do, they might not believe at all, and the freedom to choose (whether it deals with god, abortion or some other issue) is what makes it great to be human. We have free will; we have to realize that everybody else does too.

If we have free will and know all of us have the same, then fairness has to be one its key components. It is unfair to tax poor people a lot and rich people a little, even though a not so thorough investigation would reveal the opposite; that even though the poor say the rich are only taxed a small percentage (which is true), they're actually taxed a lot in dollar amounts.

The only problem is there are so many loopholes, incentives, offshore tax havens and subsidies (sometimes written by businesses or lobbyists themselves) that they don't pay them most of the time anyway. That is the ultimate unfairness, that a company or individual can earn billions of dollars in a year and pay no taxes, yet poor and working folks have no loopholes or lobbyists and are always paying more and more taxes.

When there is a deficit, who do you think the have-mores come running to take from first? They worry about their precious billions of dollars (or their manufactured opportunity of earning a billion dollars) while some of us don't have enough to eat or have a place to sleep and are forced to beg for money on the corner with our baby crying in a stroller next to us in the pouring rain; I know this is an extreme example, but you get my point. We have to come to a place where all this is a distant and unhappy memory.

We all know this exists out there; we just have to ask ourselves, what are we going to do about it?

FIRST: We have to stop blindly following our elected officials. Just because we elected somebody on campaign promises that made them sound like the bright light amidst the darkness that will carry us through to the promised land, doesn't mean they don't need to be checked on and/or pushed in the right direction.

Every great leader was only great because they had a mass movement behind them, pushing them to be better and to stick to their promises. We must push our elected officials to be accountable, to keep humanistic beliefs towards all people, and to truly represent all of us, not just a small elite group.

NUMBER 2: We must not let morals, religion, bias, intolerance, racism, economics, conspiracy theories or environmental attitudes divide us. We need to realize these things don't matter in the bigger scheme of things, and coupled with materialism are meant to keep us distracted and fighting amongst each other, so we stay oblivious to the real problems that we face as a people. We must stop getting distracted, and push the fight towards the small governing elite and show them beyond a shadow of a doubt, that their "bread and circuses" will never, ever work on us again!

NUMBER 3: We must find a way to balance the ideas of compromise, standing up for what we believe in and drawing a line in the sand promising we will fight to the bitter end. The definition of compromise seems to be when no-one is happy: sometimes, this is the solution we must come to so we can avoid bloodshed, disagreement, stalemate and/or the whole system crashing down.

The hard part is figuring out when to compromise and when to stand tall. We might figure some fight is worth fighting, or we might try to be the bigger, more conscious person and walk away or take ourselves out of the fight.

What if a law is truly unjust or a policy is unjust, or a system is unjust, doesn't being human require us to stand up with peaceful civil disobedience so we can break up and change those unjust aspects of life. We always have to be willing to compromise because it's what breeds equality of people and policy, and is the grease that keeps the gears of democracy in working order.

 We also have to be willing to fight for all of our collective and individual needs. We have to get off our asses and get out there and do something.

All of the distractions that are placed on us by the ruling elite, governmental body, business or ruling class (however you name it) are meant to prevent a critical mass they greatly fear and know in their souls that they could do nothing to stop. We must work together; we must band together; we must be relentless in our pursuit of improving the planet for all its present and future inhabitants.

We must realize that sometimes compromise is the only way out of a sticky situation; but we must also realize that sometimes we have to fight with all our courage and strength to evolve as a species and throw off our oppressors. When the time comes, what will you do?

MY ULTIMATE GOAL AS A MADMAN FOR GOOD IS TO SHOW SOMETIMES YOU HAVE TO FIGHT AND REBEL, YET ALWAYS BE CONSCIOUS TO DEFEND THE SOLUTIONS THAT WILL ACTUALLY WORK!!!!

www.ingramcontent.com/pod-product-compliance
Lightning Source LLC
Chambersburg PA
CBHW031332040426
42443CB00005B/303